FIX YOUR DRINKING PROBLEM IN 2 DAYS

D0755989

80003387047

Northamptonshire Libraries & Information Services NW	
Askews & Holts	

First published in 2008 by Five Areas.
This edition first published in 2012 by Darton, Longman and Todd Ltd
1 Spencer Court, 140–142 Wandsworth High Street, London SW18 4JJ.

Copyright © 2008 Dr Chris Williams. The right of Dr Chris Williams to be
identified as the compiler of this work has been asserted in accordance with
the Copyright, Designs and Patents Act 1998.

ISBN 978-0-232-52926-5

A catalogue record for this book is available from the British Library.
Printed and bound in Great Britain by Halstan & Co Ltd, Amersham.

Although we hope you find this book helpful, it's not intended to be a direct
substitute for consultative advice with a healthcare professional, nor does
the author or the publisher give any assurances about its effectiveness in a
particular case. Accordingly, neither the author nor the publisher shall be held
liable for any loss or damages arising from its use.

FIX YOUR DRINKING PROBLEM IN 2 DAYS

Dr Chris Williams

DARTON·LONGMAN+TODD

HOW MUCH DO YOU DRINK?

No...really.

When doctors ask this question, they add 50% to the answer because everyone underestimates their consumption.

It's seldom deliberate. What with generously filled wine glasses at home and the odd tipple after work, it's easy to lose count.

But if you're going to really fix your problem, you need a better handle on your habit.

And, at the risk of sounding like a government leaflet, we're going to use units of alcohol to do the totting up.

There's a picture chart over the page to help you work things out, but you might also like to know the theory of units, so that you can do a quick calculation when you drink something weird that's not on the list.

1 litre of a drink that's 10% Alcohol
By Volume (ABV) = 10 units.
Half a litre = 5 units.

1 litre of a drink that's 15% ABV = 15 units.
Half a litre = 7.5 units.

If a drink is 5% ABV, like a
continental lager, a litre = 5 units.

Simple!

Or you might prefer the Easy Booze Chart, overleaf!

Easy**Booze**Chart

3 UNITS — Pint of Beer or Ale

5 UNITS — Full strength Cider & Lager

2.3 UNITS — Standard glass of wine

1 UNIT — Glass of Whisky

These units are based on pub measures. When you pour yourself a whisky or a glass of wine at home, they're usually bigger, so you'd better add 20%!

Shots and Cocktails

Alcopops

Gin and Tonic

Glass of Sherry

Are you ready for your drinking diary?

Now that you know about units, it's time to add them up. Drink normally for the next seven days and fill in the diary overleaf with what you drank and the number of units you put away each day.

What I'm Drinking - Honest

	SESSION 1 WHAT I DRANK AND WHERE	SESSION 2 WHAT I DRANK AND WHERE	WHA
Example	Two pints at lunchtime 6 Units	Two glasses of wine with dinner 4.6 units	
MON			
TUE			
WED			
THU			
FRI			
SAT			
SUN			

NOW, ABOUT THOSE 2 DAYS

If you're a bit alarmed by the total units in your diary, don't worry. You can cut down easily and permanently with our 2-day method.

Here's how it works:

NO daY

Look at your drinking diary and choose the day with the smallest number of units. This is the day you're going to make into **No Day.**

That is, the one day in the week that you don't drink alcohol at all. Yes, that's right – just one day!

We're going to help you do it on the next few pages and we promise it will be easier than you think.

LO daY

Now look at your diary again and choose a second day. It could be one with fewer than average units, or the one that you feel would be easiest to make into **Lo Day.** That is, the day when you drink **half as much** alcohol as you did in your diary.

Again, we'll help you with a method that really works and doesn't hurt!

Easy method coming up

CHANGE THE WHAT, CHANGE THE WHERE

... and make it easy on yourself

WHAT you drink affects the amount of alcohol you take in.

A shandy is half as alcoholic as a lager. A glass of wine is twice as strong as a spritzer. A glass of Lambrusco is much less alcoholic than a glass of Shiraz. And soft drinks are not alcoholic at all.

So if you change WHAT you drink, you can reduce or eliminate daily units quite easily.

WHERE you drink is the other big thing you can change.

If you drink at home while watching TV, you'll cut down your intake by going out for a walk instead, or to the cinema.

If you drink at the pub, it'll be easy to stop or cut down for a day if you go somewhere else – dance classes, to see a friend, to the library, to a concert... like that.

By thinking about each drinking session in your diary and choosing the change that will be easiest to make – the WHAT or the WHERE – you'll find that fixing your drinking problem really is just a 2-day task.

And don't forget, you can mix and match WHAT and WHERE on the same day. Like Neil.

It's time you met Neil...

Now let's hear from Lisa

Choose your No Day and your Lo Day

Turn back to page **5** and pick your days. Make it easy on yourself and choose days that are already low in units for your

NO daY   and your   **LO** daY

Think about how easy it will be to change the **WHATs** and the **WHEREs** as you make your decision, and when you've settled on your days, mark them in the special column like this: ▶

Now decide on a start date and go for it!

At the end of 8 weeks, you'll be well into your new routine and will be able to fill in the 8-week column in your diary with your new daily units.

You'll have cut your alcohol consumption by around 20% and you ought to be feeling pretty chuffed with yourself!

But what if 20% isn't enough?

YOU DO IT ALL AGAIN IN 8 WEEKS TIME

The 2-day method works over and over

A 20% reduction is a great start, but if you're getting to enjoy having a clear head, you might want to reduce your drinking still further.

No problem. All you need to do is turn back to your diary, choose another **No Day** and another **Lo Day** and follow the whole process again.

Then, 8 weeks later, fill in your new units score in the spare column and give yourself a pat on the back for having fixed your drinking problem with the 2-day method!

And if you want to go on and eliminate alcohol altogether, just switch your **Lo Days** to **No Days**, change the **WHAT** and the **WHERE**, and you'll be on the wagon within a few weeks.

Don't beat yourself up about it

Nobody's perfect and even when you're cutting down just two days a week, there will probably be times when you weaken and have a crafty glug of something naughty.

The trick is not to think of it as a disaster. OK, you had a drink when you shouldn't have, or went to the pub instead of the park. Big deal.

Fixing your drinking problem is like any other habit change – it takes a few weeks to become part of your routine and there are bound to be hiccups along the way.

So give yourself a smack on the back of the hand and get back to the plan next week, increasing your motivation by reminding yourself **why** you're doing this.

SO
WHY ARE
YOU
DOING
THIS?

Whatever your reason, write it down

Take a piece of paper and make a note of why you're cutting down your drinking.

Maybe you want to live longer, to see the grandchildren graduate, to get fitter, to get a job, to keep a job, to lose some weight, to catch up with studies, to rescue a relationship…whatever your reason, write it down.

Now fold that bit of paper and keep it with you. Take it out and look at it whenever you weaken.

Next, go into the bathroom and write on the mirror with lipstick or a wax pencil. Write your reason again, where you'll see it every morning.

Now get some sticky notes and write your reason on half a dozen of them. Stick them all over the house – on the fridge, on the TV, on the bedside table, on your PC screen if you have one.

The more you remind yourself why, the less likely you will be to slip.

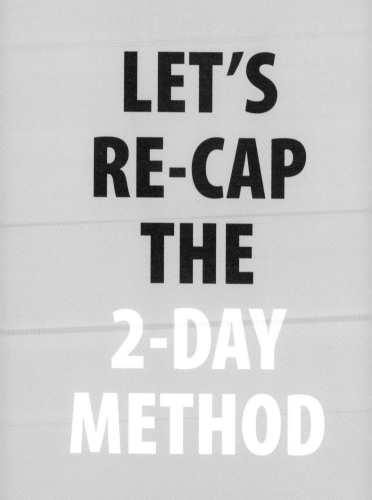

LET'S RE-CAP THE 2-DAY METHOD

1   Keep a diary for a week so you know how many units you drink every day

2   Pick the day with least units and make this into
NO daY

3   Change the **WHATs** and the **WHEREs** to make it easy

4   Now pick the second lightest day and make this into
LO daY

5   Change the **WHATs** and the **WHEREs** to make it easy

6   Pick a start date and keep it up for 8 weeks, by which time your new habits will be ingrained and you will have cut your alcohol intake by about 20%

7   If you want to cut further, choose another **No Day** and another **Lo Day** and do it all again for 8 weeks

8   If you want to stop drinking altogether, just change all remaining **Lo Days** into **No Days**.

9   If you slip, don't beat yourself up, just get back to the plan

10   Write your reason everywhere, and look at it every day

Cheers and Good Luck!

A NOTE FOR VERY HEAVY DRINKERS

If you've been a big drinker for a while, you might feel sick or sweaty or even get the shakes during your **No Day.** In this case, try two **Lo Days** instead.

If you're still feeling bad, it might be best to talk to your doctor and discuss tactics, or contact your local health service

HELP WITH OTHER PROBLEMS

This little book is one of a series by Dr Chris Williams that helps you deal with the challenges life can throw at you

There are books for low mood, anger management, low self-esteem, worry, post-natal depression and stopping smoking. There's one that can help you fix almost anything, like getting a job, making friends or getting out of debt, and there's even one that helps you lose weight and get fitter.

All the books are backed up by a website
www.livinglifetothefull.com
where you can use free audio and video courses and also connect with other people who have similar problems. You can also read the little books online at www.fiveareasonline.com

ABOUT THIS BOOK

With websites receiving over 4 million hits a month and a wealth of supporting research data, the Five Areas Approach on which this book is based, devised by Dr Chris Williams, is one of the most widely-used CBT systems in the world.

Cognitive Behavioural Therapy (CBT) has a strong evidence base for helping people with low mood, anxiety and a growing range of other common mental and physical health difficulties.

Want to learn more about you? Turn things around in your life for the better? The Five Areas Approach can help you to do this. It takes the proven CBT model and makes it accessible and practical so that you can have the tools you need to help change things in your life – fast.

Please visit the Five Areas websites – www.llttf.com (free life skills course), www.llttfshop.com (bookshop) and www.fiveareasonline.com (online books) – to discover more about this work and see the other resources on offer.

Dr Chris Williams is Professor of Psychosocial Psychiatry at the University of Glasgow, UK, and is a past-President of the British Association for Behavioural and Cognitive Psychotherapies (www.babcp.com) – the lead body for CBT in the UK, Patron of the charities Anxiety UK and Triumph over Phobia and is a well-known CBT workshop leader and researcher.

PICK ME UP

Turn your life around – fast!

Available in the Pick Me Up range:

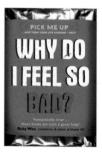

DARTON · LONGMAN + TODD

**Please visit www.dltbooks.com
for more information.**

PICK ME UP
AND TURN YOUR LIFE AROUND – FAST!

10 THINGS YOU CAN DO TO FEEL HAPPIER STRAIGHT AWAY

'Fantastically clear ... these books are such a great help!'
Ruby Wax, comedienne, & patron of Anxiety UK

PICK ME UP
AND TURN YOUR LIFE AROUND – FAST!

ARE YOU STRONG ENOUGH TO KEEP YOUR TEMPER?

'Fantastically clear ... these books are such a great help!'
Ruby Wax, comedienne, & patron of Anxiety UK

PICK ME UP
AND TURN YOUR LIFE AROUND – FAST!

STOP SMOKING IN FIVE MINUTES

'Fantastically clear ... these books are such a great help!'
Ruby Wax, comedienne, & patron of Anxiety UK

PICK ME UP
AND TURN YOUR LIFE AROUND – FAST!

I Can't Be Bothered Doing Anything

'Fantastically clear ... these books are such a great help!'
Ruby Wax, comedienne, & patron of Anxiety UK

PICK ME UP
AND TURN YOUR LIFE AROUND – FAST!

I FEEL SO BAD I CAN'T GO ON

'Fantastically clear ... these books are such a great help!'
Ruby Wax, comedienne, & patron of Anxiety UK

PICK ME UP
AND TURN YOUR LIFE AROUND – FAST!

WHY DOES EVERYTHING ALWAYS GO WRONG?

AND OTHER BAD THOUGHTS YOU CAN BEAT

'Fantastically clear ... these books are such a great help!'
Ruby Wax, comedienne, & patron of Anxiety UK